ARCHWAY's VALENTINE LOVE

Archie E. Anderson

ARCHWAY'S VALENTINE LOVE

A Mythbreaker Book

First Edition

© Copyright 2013 Archie Edgar Anderson (1917-) & Donald Murray Anderson (1950-)

All rights reserved. Without limiting rights under copyright reserved above, no part of this book may be reproduced, stored in or introduced into a retrieval system, or transmitted in any form or by any means (electronic, mechanical, photocopying, recording, or otherwise) without prior written permission of the copyright owner.

For information address: mythsbreaker@myway.com

Return of Verse

TOGETHER APART

VALENTINE FUN TIME

VALENTINES

MY VALENTINE

VALENTINE SWEETS

LOVE LOVERS

FRIENDLY LOVE

UNCONDITIONAL LOVE

Return of Verse

Could it be this verse is late?
Should I blame it all on fate?
After all, with things upset,
Can't expect a poem yet.

Though each day I had spare time,
I just had, 'a lapse of rhyme';
And perhaps too much to say –
(How could I forget the way?)

Now I feel it coming back;
In the groove, I'm on the track
Of a poem I hope is fine –
All for you, My Valentine!

TOGETHER
APART
(verses crossing space and time)

Our Tomorrow

The day is quickly nearing;
Tomorrow is in sight –
From then, we'll be appearing
Together, day and night

There'll be no further parting
When we are man and wife
For then we will be starting,
Enjoying "us" for life.

Then we'll find these months we wait
Will one scant moment seem,
When we keep our future date –
This time apart a dream.

Although we may be lonely
Until we meet once more,
It always will be "only" –
We'll never change that score!

Eternal Three

Honey, here's the problem I must face:
Heart is full of words, with none in place.
As inside my head they spin around,
No rhyme nor reason can be found.

Yet, if I should work both day and night
On verse, there'd be ever more to write
Just reminding, as I spoil for life,
How I love you, darling, sweetheart wife.
My wand is waved while I draw out three
Words, both new and old, for all to see.

And, though millions take them for their won,
We two share the trio, all alone.
Wind is wave again but nothing more,
Worth the writing, joins our perfect score.

Those sparkling three in all their glory - -

They need no help to tell their story.

Though the other threes we've shared are gone,

In our hearts one special lingers on,

Keeping pace with rhythm of each beat,

Reminding us, living will repeat.

Yes, sweet child, it always adds to show,

There may be a million words or so

But, we know that none of them will do

Or matter while we share, I love you.

Sweetheart Sketch

I gathered all the starlight
From distant reaches of the night draped skies;
But, yet, their blazing glory
Shone dim beside the sparkle of your eyes.

I collected gossamer,
Those fairy tracings of a peaceful air,
But, the finest was too coarse
When I beheld soft halo of your hair.

I drew the gods' fine nectar,
Enough to float at least a thousand ships,
But it could never equal
One single honeyed sip from your sweet lips.

I picked shells from seven seas,
And sorted every color, shape and shade;

But found none that could compare

With symmetry of charm your ears have made.

I searched for softer tones

Amid the noise and echoes of the earth;

But the pick of music's beat

Fell far short beside your voice's dulcet worth.

I'll return to you some day

With details of a full report complete,

But you may quote me always,

You are my darling, sweetest of the sweet.

May I___?

We'll dance on roof of world

And greet a happy moon,

On the night that follows

Tomorrow's afternoon.

And as we glide along,

We'll laugh at everyone;

Screwball people having

A screwball time – but fun.

Though others shake their heads

And think that we are mad,

We'll laugh again, at us,

And for our 'state' be glad.

But then, we'll steal away

'Til music whispers low,

And have ourselves alone,

To speak of things we know.

Our thanks for all that is

Will fill the peaceful night;

For days that end with "us"

Will be forever right.

So, rest your feet, dear wife

Until I call back there

To take you in my arms,

And dance you everywhere.

Number One - My Wife

My heart's off to my darling wife,
　　Sweet gal I left behind;
At taking care of husband's heart,
　　None better could you find

No matter where the warpath leads,
　　She's always by my side
To take my hand in memory - -
　　Inspiring, lovely guide.

Take all the paper on this earth
　　And use last drop of ink;
The words they write could never tell,
　　Dear sweetheart, what I think.

There can never be a question,
　　Of all both big and small,

To bother while there's honey child.

She's answer to them all.

Each lonely day and night apart

Adds to the growing pile

As thoughts of Hazel prop my chin

And bring the brightest smile.

So that's just how it is, my dear,

(In case you never knew),

No other man will ever have

A wife as nice as you.

One From One

How are things at home my dear?

Is the sky still blue and clear,

Or has it a sombre hue

Since I've not been there with you?

Do the birds all sing as sweet,

Or is theirs a mournful tweet?

How about the hits they swing?

Have they still that joyful ring?

And, those frosty Fridays child;

Do they seem a trifle mild

When the early morning view

Is by one instead of two?

Do you ever, just by chance,

Steal a hopeful sideways glance?

As the actors show their best,

Does it lack a certain zest?

On a busy, crowded street,

Through the noise of countless feet,

Is there echo from the past –

Shades of time we walked there last?

And, most of all, do you feel

Time apart cannot be real?

If you do, before you start,

Like the answers from my heart.

Smear Nothing Dear

Honey, after all I've said,
Once again you smear the red
Tell me, what have you to say,
Making it 'pink' letter day?

I've been patient, I've been kind
But, sweetheart please, do you mind
Getting chapter sealing grip?
Stop that mark of crimson lip.

But, don't get me wrong, or think
Such a color makes me shrink
After all, there are places –
I do mean heads, not faces.

Scarlet smudge on letter flap
Does bring shades of girl meets chap,

But I wonder, once again,

If my coaching was in vain.

Could it be that you forget

Our first date that was all wet,

When I really looked at you

With no paint to spoil my view?

Added up, it comes to this –

Save that trace of paper kiss;

I should rather, can't you see,

Have your fresh paint mark on me.

Simply Simply

In my dreams no charpoy, but instead,

Soft and roomy comfort, pukkah bed.

And no net to close me in at night

With no winged or other pests to bite

Pure water from a tap without fear

Any deadly germs are lurking near

Which lay more low where pani runs

Then fell beneath weight of bombs or guns

From the rotee spotted dirty gray

I'll turn soon some bright and happy day.

Whether it be white or brown, each slice

Will be cheap at almost any price

Oh to fill my lungs with deepest breath

And yet not risk quick and choking death

Oh to stand and sniff each fragrant breeze

And find no stench brings a cough or sneeze.

And to simply walk where skins are pale

Or see half a million folks and fail

To find one, in any crowd I meet,

Not dressed up in style of civy street.

But one dream I cherish most of all

For each summer, winter, spring and fall

Line between job and private life

When we are together, darling wife.

Remember Us?

Remember 'way back when
Spoil by poetry was new.
The tease was red heads then –
Sometimes I wonder – do you?

Remember how we had
Build up great that's with us yet
And how the words all led
On to love from day we met

Remember splash around
First "in lieu of tennis" night
How it shook when you found
My hair lay flat alright.

Remember how, by gate,
All our goodnights started out, sweet,

And how each weekend date

Was our extra special treat.

Remember first New Year

Lips clung close for silent score –

You voiced our thoughts my dear

With that simple whisper, "more".

Remember, tomorrow,

We collect from life, arrears,

Nor allow a borrow

From our time in million years.

Love Letters

In moment first of future day

Life complete will arrive, to stay

On and never cease while we share

Vital score, telling how we care.

Each second will belong to us,

Yet never lose the fresh, sweet fun

Of perfect spoil in person, hon.,

Until there sets, forever's sun.

Don't ever change, from gal I knew

Away back when affection grew,

Rising as we wrote build up page,

Let's keep our minds in sweetheart stage

It's what you are, my chosen one,

Not anything you might have done;

Growing in my heart as flower,

Holds promise for each future hour

Always, for living full, I need

Zest your presence adds to each deed

"Ever" will start from day we meet;

Lasting for keeps, at least, my sweet.

Delight in forever finding

Extra reasons for reminding

All things you mean from year to year,

Reveals a precious total clear -

Tomorrow Brings

Tomorrow brings a moon which we can share

When star friends rendezvous with it so bright

And add their sparks to fill the night dulled air

With punctuation marks of moon's soft light.

Tomorrow brings our dreams and hopes to life.

As we laugh, props for chins are thrown away,

No longer needed; happy man and wife,

We want no more than us for every day.

Tomorrow brings the promise of an end

To all the days and nights we are apart,

And ushers in a future we can spend

Just spoiling us the "two please" way, sweetheart.

Tomorrow brings the answer that will suit –

Our wait will be forever done and past

As future turns to present; we salute

A life and happy love we know will last.

Tomorrow brings to us very much

Of all the things we know are full worth while,

We'll carry on with paper chapter crutch,

And never once forget that we can smile.

Tomorrow brings us close together, sweet,

For our hold tight, where whisper faint will do

To bring that same old thrill as we repeat

That ever fresh and perfect, I love you.

Rolling On – Unquote

We draw a bead on future
As if drifts before our sights,
And we know it will reward
Vigil of those lonely nights.

A misty dawn is breaking
With tomorrow coming fast,
Bringing promise that our wait
Is to be forever past.

As duration ink runs low,
We know that we never will,
Need another one, my dear,
After love and life refill.

Duty watch is on the run,
But memory will remain

Of those happy Portage days,

As we fall in love again.

Adding up the living cost,

For prices have gained much;

Parting lesson soon will give

Days we share an extra touch.

So knock away the chin props,

Lay aside our paper scrawl,

On the day that we have us –

But forever, only, all.

Score's Encore

Sad or happy, all the same

I'm the guy, you're the dame

Who get such fun from giving

Us sweet joy - perfect living.

We've kept both chins in place;

(Yes, I mean one chin per face).

We've not lost a single smile,

Nor let war cramp happy style.

From our happy side by side

To half a world, lonely wide,

We obeyed war lords command,

Played as fate had dealt our hand.

Struggling through a weary night,

In our dreams we held us tight,

Knowing that our day would dawn

And long duty watch be gone.

Time is near to open eyes,

Bid goodbye to wistful sighs,

Find our place in our own book,

Live without a backward look.

Our tomorrow's due to start

And the song that fills each heart,

As we wait for final cue,

Begins and ends "I love you".

Last Valentine Apart

Could be same old sweetheart line,

One and only Valentine,

Yet it's always fresh and new

As, each time, I offer you

Heart and all that stands for me

Yours, a lifetime, two or three

And, no matter where I roam,

You keep safe my heart, at home,

On soft cushion of your love,

Which I know is far above

Whisper of a shadow's doubt;

Pure white flame that won't go out.

Hearts around the world we've been,

For an uncompleted scene

On three days of Valentine,

But, we've had our thoughts in line

And know present lonely lane

Leads to life and love again

Polish up that same old moon,

Set the stage for two, but soon

(Honey, need I tell you why?)

It's official from the guy

Who is coming back to stay,

Dear Valentine, every day.

(MANY, MANY YEARS LATER…)

Perpetual Valentines

On this day for lovers all,

We recall our first one when;

World at war thrust us apart;

But Valentines even then.

Many things have changed

Since Valentine first love we gave.

But we know there'll always be

Something we will always save.

True Valentines we will be,

Each year on this special day.

But our love will carry on

Day by day in every way.

Year-round Valentines

For more than a hundred years

Loving Valentines we have been;

But not for just a day a year.

Each day has been a loving scene.

How long we have we cannot tell,

There is, we know, one thing certain;

True Valentines we'll ever be,

Until at least final curtain.

We've celebrated year by year;

Though World War Two some years did snatch.

Was no more than pause as we soon

Shared life again with our love match.

VALENTINE FUN TIME

Of Valentines

I sit and think upon this day

Of many things that I could say.

Roses are red it is quite true,

But look and see the white ones too.

Though violets are blue, I hear,

To me it always did seem queer

That in this should-be-happy time

They use that blue to make it rhyme.

That sugar's sweet I do not doubt.

But one thing I'm not clear about

Is why I can't in one short line

Say, "Will you be my Valentine?"

Leap Year Valentine

Now, girls, it seems to me

When thinking of you three,

There are things which should be done.

But to act I'm not the one.

Of course this should not seem so queer

Since Nineteen Forty is the year.

No, I don't think I need

To say, "You take the lead."

If at times I hint to you,

It's to show you what to do.

Just pause and read between these lines --

Remember there are Valentines!

The Valentines should go

The other way you know.

Cards I send you just in case--

No need even to erase.

Besides my name you may write, "To"

And underneath say it's from you.

Valentine Truce

It's true I've said you are a brat,

But just for now we'll skip all that.

Then everything will be just fine

Upon this day of Valentine.

For Leap Year things are turned around;

But I will give a little ground;

I will supply a verse or two --

The Valentine is up to you!

Roses are <u>Red</u>

To make our Valentine complete

And also sweep you off your feet,

I've bought a box for me – not you

A square one and of lovely blue.

My poem is no more than rhyme

If you should wish then add a line

And my surprise is red on time

Will you be my Valentine.

To Two Valentines

That day I scarce' believed my eyes
When at night I saw my mail.
It was indeed a great surprise,
(Though I hoped you would not fail).

I say the pleasure is all mine,
But it does not seem so queer
From each to get a Valentine --
Nineteen Forty is Leap Year.

Will you two girls excuse conceit
If this I confess to you?
Should this keep up 'twill be a feat
To escape when all pursue!

I thank you for the Valentines
On that day from you to me.
I had to write these grateful lines
Which can stand in memory.

Unfinished Love

He held her close, she breathed a sigh.

He vowed for her he'd gladly die.

His arms drew tight about her waist;

He wondered how her lips would taste.

As they stood, holding cheek to cheek,

He nerved himself a kiss to sneak.

He slowly edged his lips around;

She sighed again but gave no ground.

He turned to her in mute appeal.

Her look he saw invited, 'steal'.

He drew her close and thought, "At last!"

His lips touched hers – stepped back aghast.

He turned from her in bitter scorn.

Now listen ladies while I warn:

Don't let this thing your love usurp --

No man on earth will kiss a burp!

Precious Valentines

For sweet Valentines, man did look,

But not just one, or even two.

Indeed it was his fondest wish

To have at least more than a few.

He was not greedy as it seems.

Nor thought more than one encumbers.

He, after all, felt quite sure

There was safety great in numbers.

When there were many Valentines,

Thought easy then to pick and choose.

If one he lost then more were left.

It did seem, no way he could lose.

But this silly man soon found out,

His plans ended quite abrupt.

The cost of Valentines was high.

He lost them all and went bankrupt.

VALENTINES

Some Valentines

Am looking for sweet valentines,

But not just one, or even two.

Indeed it is my fondest wish

To have at least more than a few.

Am not even one bit greedy;

Don't think more than once encumbers.

You, after all, should surely know

There is safety great in numbers.

When there are many Valentines,

It's easy then to pick and choose.

If one you lose then more are left.

There's really no way you can lose.

Valentine unlimited

Oh Valentine so sweet,

Upon this happy day,

Do hope you will agree

To send a smile my way.

There is a problem slight

You may not be aware;

Some other Valentines

This special day must share.

So, be My Valentine;

Let's hope you're not too proud

To find you are, indeed,

One Valentine in crowd.

Mrs. Miss Ms. Valentine?

The yearly search is on,
Sweet Valentines abound;
Who knows for certain sure
Where true love will be found.

Everyone's a sweetheart
Upon this special day;
All girls are Valentines;
The young to sometime grey.

Here are some spicy hearts;
Hope the symbol's fitting.
Please be my Valentine –
Women's Lib permitting.

True Valentine

Sweethearts by the millions
Pledge Valentines today,
Promising each other
True love for every day.

Candy, hearts and flowers
Attest that Valentine
Is a special sweetheart,
A person so divine.

True test of Valentine
Is not too hard to tell;
Sweetheart on fourteenth,
And rest of year as well.

Valentine Days

Saint Valentine was on right track
When he pledged love to all,
No matter young or old and gray,
Short or fat, lean or tall.

One day each year the world is full
Of love in name of Saint,
With cards and blooms, and candy sweet,
Plus streaking cupids quaint.

So pledge your Valentine this year,
To chosen one be true;
You should keep loving Valentine
At least the whole year through.

Valentines For All

Saint Valentine, it is said,

Spread love and hope everywhere.

His message was for all the year;

Each day tell others that you care.

Lovers, of course, have special place,

But love is shared by many more.

It can range from so very mild

To point where others you adore.

Be sure to tell each Valentine,

Though love you share with quite a few,

Each and every one is unique,

With love to you, and you, and you.

Here's to all you Valentines.

Very young to very old;

Keep the fire burning bright:

And never let your love grow cold.

Valentine Days

To all happy Valentines,

From most young to most mature,

This greeting's for you, and you.

Hope your love may long endure.

Spririt of Saint Valentine

In this world that's so upset,

Is most surely needed now.

Let love good example set.

Valentines should always be

Treated as a treasure dear,

Not just for their special day,

But every day, every year.

Valentine Hope

When we do think of Valentines,

Should link the loving Saint to

The one with love for everyone;

Pluto, who should receive his due.

If we could only join the two

And subdue all the world-wide hate,

There would be hope for human kind.

So, let's spread love before too late.

If you believe in Valentines,

Then, every moment of the year,

Let others share loving moments

As Valentines so very dear.

MY VALENTINE

Just my Valentine

Why should I pick you

To be my Valentine?

Why should your agree

Forever to be mine?

Reason is quite clear,

My Valentine Sweetheart;

And it will not change,

Together or apart.

Day of Valentine

Has many memories dear,

And we'll always be

Sweet Valentines all year.

Soul Valentine

You are my Valentine,

Of that there is no doubt,

Always know you'll be mind,

No matter who's about.,

All my love, Valentine,

Is yours throughout the year,

But on this day of love

It seems you are more dear.

Oh Valentine, you are

Most precious sweet delight;

Love you every moment

Throughout each day and night.

So, here's to Valentine;

Each day I discover

New reasons to be glad

You're my sweetheart lover.

True Valentine

We have been our Valentines

For thirty years, and more;

And each year upon this day

Renew our loving score.

We've always known that our love

Really knows no season;

Love upon a Valentine

Is but extra reason.

So, about our Valentines,

There's not much more to say,

As you are my Valentine

For now and every day.

True Valentines

Though it seems many years

Since first we spoke of love,

It remains ever fresh,

As dew drops from above.

You are my Valentine,

Of that there is not doubt.

Though words I must whisper,

Within my heart I shout.

May not be together

On lovers' special day;

But we'll know that we are

True Valentines to stay.

Full-Time Valentine

You've been my Valentine

For thirty years, and more;

And it seems you're sweeter

Each Valentine encore.

To you, my Valentine,

And all our love imparts,

You'll always be for me

My precious Queen of Hearts.

I know you'll always be

My special Valentine,

Whatever time of year,

Come rain, or cloud, or shine.

Thirty Love

You have been my Valentine

For thirty years, and more;

And now we add another

To ever loving score.

If day is just like others

It simply goes to show

We know without reminding

Our daily love does grow.

Sweet and precious Valentine,

Today and every day

You will be my Valentine,

And always stay that way.

Our Share

Couples live together

But somehow drift apart.

Side by side in body

But klicks away in heart.

If it is one-sided

Then absence is the best

With freedom for the one

Who'd like to shake a pest.

Perhaps there's only one

The other doesn't care.

But love will never change

No matter when nor where.

We learnt from beginning

That true love is to share,

And we are together,

A living, loving pair.

Perfect Valentine

On Saint Valentines some give

Precious gifts, and sweet ones too;

Which may make you wonder what

This day has in store for you.

Could give sweets and flowers too.

But they so soon pass away.

Something precious that we share

That will last from day to day.

It's a gift that never fails,

And will last as long as life;

Gift of love I offer you,

My Valentine and my wife.

Our Valentine

Since we picked us as Valentine
So many heart beats throbbed away;
And still our love is ever fresh
As we together face each day.

So great to be your Valentine
For every moment, every year.
Our love is something that we share
As sweetheart Valentines so dear.

We know, as we live heart to heart
There'll never be the need of sign
To prove we have a precious love
That means each day is Valentine.

Valentine Gift

Our sweethearts' day is here once more,

As our love we renew;

Not Valentines for just one day,

But lovers whole year through.

We need no special day to show

How much we both do care,

As every day we live and love,

And precious time we share.

If able to give many gifts

To rival stars above,

Not one of them could ever match

Most perfect gift of love.

Valentines – Plus

Upon this day of Valentines,

No matter near or far apart,

By young and by old, love is shared

As lovers pledge from heart to heart.

One special day when most take part

With gifts of flowers, sweets, and more,

But then relax throughout the year.

For them Valentines yearly chore.

You are my Valentine, each day,

And every day, for every year;

As Valentine and love are ours;

Valentine - Plus

My Valentine you'll always be;

You are the only one for me.

Very precious love we do share;

Always is and shall ever be.

Love which started on tennis court,

Each day we know has been renewed.

Never has our love been in doubt.

The time has passed as we reviewed

It, and answer always is the same,

Now we can look back and claim,

Each day, now and then, is the same.

Valentine Spirit

In these days of stress and strife,

Saint Valentine would be

Upset by the lack of love,

In this world, for you and me.

So, in the day for sweethearts;

Young and old, we should reach out

And show others that we care;

That's what love is all about.

Spirit of Saint Valentine

Guides every hug, kiss and smile;

Not just for a single day

All year love should be in style.

True Valentines

Send Valentines to others
Each year, as you know I do;
But, of course, there is no doubt,
Only Valentine is you.

We have happy memories of
Days of Valentine we shared;
Though needed no reminder
To show how much we both cared.

Upon this day for sweethearts,
Each pair's love is pledged anew;
But our love continues on –
Valentines the whole year through.

VALENTINE SWEETS

Especially For You

For all my Valentines

Upon this special day,

There is a special gift,

Some special words to say.

Though heart I dare not share

With each and every dear,

For Day of Valentine

I must make feelings clear.

Here's a sweet solution,

Sweet Valentines for you;

Take my heart by dozens - -

To each of you I'm true.

Sweet Valentines

Though legend of Saint Valentine
May be quite obscure,
The legacy of constant love
Flows forever pure.

To you, fair Valentines, so sweet,
Comes this special note
In memory of Saint Valentine,
Extra special quote.

Of course there is one Valentine,
Sweetest one, it's true,
But, still, I know that I must share
Few sweet hearts with you.

Sweet Hearts

V alentine, I bring to you

A few sweet hearts; hope they do

L et you know how much I dare.

E ach Valentine, picked with care,

N eeds no words to show I'm true.

T ake these symbols, spicy red,

I n sweet token, words unsaid.

N o Valentine more sincere;

E very one for every dear

S hows that sweet love must be fed.

Sweet Stones

I gave you polished pebbles
At party in the past;
They are the ones, which for sure,
Will last, and last, and last.

Here's a change of pace for you,
Assorted bunch of stones;
If heap of them fell on you
There'd be no broken bones.

You can view them for awhile,
Display them if you wish;
And when you've finished looking,
Just eat them off the dish.

Thank You -- ?

Oh secret Valentine

Accept my thanks for treats;

You are a thoughtful one

To ply me thus with sweets.

Could thank you in person

If I weren't in the dark;

And yet I'm sure your name

Is not a question mark.

Though I can make a guess

How can I really know

Who such sweet person is,

From whom the sweet things Flo?

Valentine Treat

Upon this day of hearts and sighs

I want you all to know

Your are my favourite Valentines –

This verse will tell you so.

Although a certain Valentine

Does have a prior claim,

Please make me happy and agree;

Play hearts and candy game.

Hope Saint Valentine's great love

Whole world today entwines

That's why I offer, in his name,

Sweet hearts, sweet Valentines.

From The Heart

May these dainty hearts

Give you much pleasure;

May they always be

Gift you can treasure.

Until happy time

We do meet once more;

Of two hearts will dream,

And love they stand for.

And, no matter what,

One thing is for sure;

In my heart you will

Ever be secure.

Sweet Hearts

V alentine, I bring to you

A few sweet hearts; hope they do

L et you know how much I dare.

E ach Valentine, picked with care,

N eeds no words to show I'm true.

T ake these symbols, spicy red,

I n sweet token, words unsaid.

N o Valentine more sincere;

E very one for every dear

S hows that sweet love must be fed.

Especially For You

Love verse to write, just for you.

Hope it always gives a lift

Do also like to surprise

When for you include a gift.

Like often to remind you,

There'll ever be special place

Reserved for you, special one;

Far away or face to face.

There is only one regret,

Which I'm sure you understand.

So dearly wish that each verse

Could give by voice or by hand.

E.S.P.

Some say E.S.P. is a gift,

The ultimate, they say.

But, from here, have a different view.

Something as plain as day.

For me, the letters do not mean

What many people think.

It is, by far, more personal;

And it's a happy link.

When you see letters E.S.P.

Here's what I hang verse on;

I think of you, and what you are;

Extra Special Person.

LOVE

LOVERS

All Valentines

Valentines are, for young to old,

A loving blessing to behold.

Lots of love, with hugs and kisses;

Each year does bring best wishes,

New romances sometimes start

To those enjoying Cupid's dart

It's wonderful so many care;

Nice knowing that people share,

Enjoying special day so dear;

So let's have love throughout the year.

Lovers

Love can be a special word,
Or mean not much at all,
As when you're playing tennis
And keep on missing ball.

Some have love for food and drink,
Some have love for singing;
Some have love for T.V. screen,
Some have love for swinging.

You'll see many kinds of love
Wherever you may look;
Some of them you never will
Find written in a book.

The love of man and woman,
Unique without a doubt;
Some so easily fall in - -
And easily fall out.

Love 'Em – But

Man, it seems, has choice

To love one or all.

Number in between

Brings about his fall.

Lucky Adam had

Everything his way;

He loved one and all

Every single day.

But Henry the Eighth

While still in his prime

Made love to them all –

Just one at a time.

Henry had a plan

To love only one,

With a quick discard

When he had to run.

Here's to "Women's Lib",

They know why and when

And may each of them

Love a million men.

A Loving Way

As you know, love has many forms;

Some of which are hard to define.

But, special love I have for you,

Will always be sweet and benign.

Though moments that we share are brief,

They're full of love and good wishes,

Each time we hold each other close,

And seal our love with kisses.

Love for you has no ifs or buts;

It is an understanding love.

Will never harm by word or deed;

Our bond is a precious gift from above.

For Love

Love, so old, but forever new,

Spreads gentle magic everywhere.

Both young and old and in between

Ignite love when they truly care.

There are so many forms of love;

From parents' love of precious child

To special love enjoyed by few,

Which makes other loves seem so mild.

Some loves don't last, just fade away.

There seems to be no reason why.

True love can last as long as life,

If every day both lovers try.

FRIENDLY
LOVE

Near And Dear

Each Sunday is extra special,

Since happy time met certain one.

Often thing of that first meeting,

And what a friendship web we've spun.

What started out as just "buddies"

Soon evolved into closer bond;

Has now become a rendezvous.

It's as if we share magic wand.

Although most weeks meet together,

In years we are quite far apart.

It is my dearest hope that we

Remain close in each other's heart.

Next Hug

You are so hugable,

In case you didn't know.

The one complaint I have,

Last one too long ago.

Can't send hug by letter,

By 'phone or internet.

Know there must be some way,

But haven't found one yet.

Will have to settle for

Memory of hug or two,

And dream of the next time

I have arms around you.

Only For Ever

This most tiny symbol of

My platonic love for you

Is offered as reminder

Of bond that's shared by we two.

Hope we always will be near

In spirit, no matter what,

As we go our separate ways;

But, daily, meet with each thought.

Perpetual Valentine

Valentines come in pairs,

While two hearts beat as one,

From Saint Valentine,

With love for everyone.

This month for lovers all

Is often cold and bleak,

But you'll find your true love

If you know where to seek.

Loving Saint led the way,

To show that love is found

Everywhere, and it's true,

Love makes the world go 'round.

Please be my Valentine,

No matter when or where;

Every day, every year.

For you I'll always care.

Precious Four

Four letter words are good and bad,

But not all used for swearing.

In fact, there's more than one of two

That show a lot of caring.

For special mention there are two;

Without limits is their scope.

They always will lead all the rest.

They are, of course, love and hope.

When there is love, there's always hope.

May our love be always strong,

And hope be always kept alive

Until our day comes along.

Sunday Sweetheart - Plus

I have so sweet Sunday Sweetheart
Who shares precious hug and a kiss
Thought just short time ago we met,
Daughter surrogate brings bliss.

From that fateful day when we met,
Our loving friendship grew apace.
Each Sunday morning when we meet,
We pledge our love as we embrace.

And, as we hold hands, hug and kiss,
Each meeting does give great pleasure.
Though so brief moments we do share,
Memories of each one we treasure.

May we ever hold each other dear;
But one thing we know cannot be:
A single taste in garden, of
Forbidden fruit for you and me.

Valentine Wish

Know Valentines you will receive.
It's nice to see how others care.
May many loving wishes, and,
Kind thoughts of love be yours to share.
Only hope, always there'll be room,
Regardless of life you lead,
So busy; hope can find the time
To be my Valentine - - in deed.

Plato's Pledge

Poets quite often write of love,

Love, they're known to claim, conquers all

And, as Plato did rightly state,

There is a love beyond recall:

One we can share and freely give;

Nor be afraid to feelings show

It is the spiritual love,

Called "platonic" as you all know.

UNCONDITIONAL LOVE

Once Upon A Valentine

Once upon a Valentine

Love was sweet and simple thing

Boy meets girl, and al is fine.

Love is sealed with wedding ring.

Now Valentines, love and life

Are never quite as they were

Couples live, not man and wife

Some men live with him, not her.

So Valentines often can

As Females who with to share

Or a man with other man

As Valentines make odd pair.

Here's to whom it may concern

Please say yes, my Valentine

You're the one for whom I yearn

Man or woman will be fine.

Here's to all you Valentines

Hims and Hers and In-betweens

All of you who have designs

On some other kings or queens.

Valentines have no reason

To fear censor or a hex

Now free love is in season

Male, female, or other sex.

Writings from Mythbreaker:

Archway series:

Archway: Six Year Book of Dreams (Vol. I)
Archway: Six Year Book of Dreams (Vol. II)
Archway: Lifetime Rhyme (Vol. I)
Archway: Lifetime Rhyme (Vol. II)
Archway's Christmas New Years Rhymes
Archway's Valentine Love
Archway's Garden Rhymes

Terrian Journals series:

A Sketch of Terrian History
Terrian Journals: Living as a Newcomer
Middle Earth Journals
Rediscovery Journals
Fukurokuju No Kasumi Journals
Sabbatical Journals
Departure Journals
Terrian Journals for the Misguided
Terrian Journals' N.S.R.: Not Spying, …Really!
TJ JNG: Terrian Journals' Jokes Nobody Gets
Terrian Journals First Anthology
Terrian Journals Second Anthology
Terrian Journals (periodical)

www.ingramcontent.com/pod-product-compliance
Lightning Source LLC
Chambersburg PA
CBHW061326040426

42444CB00011B/2791